The Schools of Barking

The Schools of Barking

Prepared and compiled by
Barking Borough Council

Valence House Publications

Published in 2022 by Valence House Publications
Valence House, Becontree Avenue
Dagenham, Essex RM8 3HT

www.valencehousecollections.co.uk

ISBN 978-1-911391-11-1

This is a facsimile reprint of The Schools of Barking originally produced in 1932 by Barking Borough Council.

Introduction and all editorial material copyright ©Valence House Publications 2022.

All rights reserved. No part of this book may be reproduced or transmitted in any form or by any means, electronic or mechanical, including photocopying, recording or by any information storage or retrieval system, without permission from the Publisher in writing.

Cover Images :
Scan of original 1932 book produced by Barking Borough Council.

Opening of New Schools :

The Director outlined the programme for the opening of the new schools on the 6th October 1932, by Sir Henry Haddow, and stated that he would recommend to the Education Committee that it should be followed by an "Open Day" to be held on the 7th October in all schools, and that a school holiday should be given on the Tuesday following the mid-term break.
(Sep 1932 EM 543)

Review of the Year (Apr-Nov 1931):

Education – I must draw attention to the heavy task of the Council in connection with the provision of schools on the Becontree Estate due to the rapid development of that portion of Barking. The work of erecting these schools is being carried out by direct labour, under the supervision of the Borough Engineer & Surveyor. Two schools, namely Erkenwald and Roding are partly completed and occupied and the temporary portions of two schools, namely Dawson and Monteagle, are completed. Commencement on another school is contemplated. It will, therefore, be seen that an endeavour is being made to provide adequate educational facilities for the children.

Mayors Report November 1932:

Education – I would, however, be lacking in my duty if I did not draw attention to the provision of schools to meet the demands of the large population now residing on the LCC Becontree Housing Estate, since 1929, 5 new schools have been erected by the Council on this estate and on the 6th October last, Sir Henry Haddow opened the following schools: Cambell, Dawson, Erkenwald, Monteagle and Roding. At present tenders are being considered for the erection of Dorothy Barley School. It will therefore be seen that the Council are fully alive to the necessity of providing adequate educational facilities for the children in this portion of the district.

THE SCHOOLS OF BARKING

A brief survey, with photographs and plans, issued on the occasion of the formal opening of the Eastbury, Cambell, Erkenwald, Roding, Dawson and Monteagle Schools by

SIR HENRY HADOW, C.B.E.,
M.A., D.Mus., Ll.D., D.Litt, F.R.C.M.,

on 6th October, 1932.

J. COMPTON, M.A.,
Director of Education.

EDUCATION COMMITTEE.

Councillor W. J. PARKER, *Chairman of the Committee*.

Councillor J. STEDMAN, J.P, *Vice-Chairman of the Committee*.

Alderman A. E. MARTIN, J.P., E.C.C., *Mayor*.

Alderman J. T. SANDERS, J.P., C.A., *Deputy Mayor*.

Alderman J. W. GARLAND, O.B.E., J.P.
„ D. G. HARDWICK.

Alderman S. B. HEARN.
„ Mrs. B. E. JACKSON

Councillor W. R. BAKER.
„ W. S. BARRETT.
„ A. BLAKE.
„ D. P. BLOOMFIELD.
„ A. EDWARDS.
„ A. G. D. GLENNY.
„ A. GRAHAM.
„ T. H. F. HOBDAY.

Councillor W. J. JAMES, J.P., C.C.
„ F. MARTIN.
„ B. PALMER.
„ F. H. PYNER.
„ H. A. RAINBOW.
„ J. W. G. REDMAN.
„ H. C. SUCKLING.
„ A. WHITING, J.P.

H. ANDERSON, Esq.
Rev. Canon V. CAMERON.
Mrs. M. A. E. CARVELL.
Rev. C. E. CHARLESWORTH.

Mrs. R. GRAHAM.
W. A. HOWE, Esq.
W. B. REIDIE, Esq.
Rev. Canon H. C. ROBINS.

P. C. VESEY, Esq.

OFFICIALS.

S. A. JEWERS, Solicitor	Town Clerk.
W. T. COCKLE, F.I.M.T.A. ...	Borough Treasurer.
R. A. LAY, Assoc.M.INST.C.E. ...	Borough Engineer and Surveyor.
W. E. KIDNER, A.M.I.E.E. ...	Borough Electrical Engineer.
C. L. WILLIAMS, B.Sc., M.R.C.S., D.P.H.	Medical Officer of Health.
C. J. DAWSON, F.R.I.B.A.	Architect.

Eastbury Senior School. View across a Quadrangle.

*Bifrons School (School "L").
Senior Boys and Girls.
Principal Entrance.*

FOREWORD.

*I*T is with great pleasure that I accede to the request to write an introductory note to this booklet which is a very interesting record of the development of educational facilities in Barking. It gives me an opportunity of expressing deep appreciation of those who have brought to a successful issue the provision of schools for the new inhabitants of our town. High in this list are Mr. J. Compton, the Director of Education, Mr. C. J. Dawson, the Architect, and Mr. R. A. Lay, the Borough Surveyor. I desire also to express the thanks of the Committee to the Officers of the Board of Education, who, realising the immensity of the problems with which the Barking Authority were faced, helped in every way they could.

The development of the Becontree Estate has placed a heavy responsibility on the inhabitants of Barking, but fortunately our townspeople have been equal to the occasion, and a culminating point is reached with the formal opening by Sir Henry Hadow of six new schools. The opening of such a number at one and the same time may well be regarded as an event of great significance in the life of an Education Committee and of the town it serves.

Barking has every reason to feel proud of these handsome and up-to-date buildings, and we all hope that they will prove to be places of light and learning which will send out into the world many generations of good men and women.

W. J. PARKER,
Chairman of the Education Committee.

Eastbury Senior School. View from Playing Fields.

Eastbury Infants' School.

The
Development of the Education Service

Retrospect. Few towns in England can be so old and yet so new as Barking. The original charter of her Abbey dates back over 1,200 years, while nearly half her present population is the product of the last ten years. When viewing the new schools to-day it is well to remember that there is a heritage from the past which tells how our forefathers shouldered the burden of educational progress.

The Abbey was probably Barking's first school, and though no record exists of its educational work for the townsfolk, we know that in 1436 King Henry VI sent Edmund and Jasper Tudor to the Abbess to be brought up in her custody, and that in 1440 the Abbess complained that £15 12s. 0d. was due for their maintenance. Even royal school bills were not always promptly paid. A hundred years later, Edmund Tudor's grandson, Henry VIII, dissolved the Abbey, and Barking was left school-less until Sir James Cambell endowed a Free School in 1642. Sir James, who was Lord Mayor of London in 1629, Warden of the Ironmongers' Company and Alderman of Billingsgate, expressed the wish before he died to found a free school in Barking, a wish that was fulfilled by his executors. The school and masters' house were probably built by 1649, in North Street, beyond the Bull Inn which dates from the same time. It was endowed with an income of £20 a year from lands in Yorkshire, and the boys were taught reading, cyphering and the rudiments of grammar. This "free school" as Cambell's Bequest was called, was still working in 1696, but late in the 18th century it was reported to be in bad condition and of little use to the parish. Times had

Eastbury Senior School. Girls' Quadrangle.

Eastbury Infants' School.

changed; workhouses, not schools, were the need of the day, so in 1787 the old school buildings were destroyed and an up-to-date workhouse erected in their place. This building still stands and is now used for shops and dwellings. In this workhouse a master and mistress were employed to teach the poor children, the expenses being met from the £20 received annually from the Cambell Bequest.

The Church Schools. For twenty years this room in the workhouse was Barking's school. Those years saw great changes. England alone was defying Napoleon, the power of steam had come to stay, the Sunday-school movement had arisen as a force in the land, and the Church of England, quickened to new enthusiasm by the rise of nonconformity, had become the leading educational pioneer. Barking was not slow to feel the stirring of the times. A Committee was formed on June 10th, 1810, to consider means of extending a Christian education to a greater number of the poor of the parish. It was resolved to establish Sunday and Charity Schools and subscriptions were invited. Within a few months the money had been collected and a school for twenty boys and twenty girls opened. The master and mistress were paid £15 and £10 per year, respectively, with £5 5s. 0d. extra for teaching at the Sunday-school. The children were clothed by the Committee, the boys in a coat, waistcoat and coloured leather breeches costing 19s. 0d., hats costing 2s. 0d., shoes at 5s. 9d. a pair, and stockings at 1s. 3d., making a total cost of £1 8s. 0d. The girls had cloaks provided at 4s. 6d. to 5s. 0d. each. Thus was founded the Church of England School. Numbers grew apace: the introduction of monitors in 1811 made it possible to double the children without increasing the staff, so that in 1827 new accommodation for 200 boys and 200 girls was required. A room, 60' × 27' × 12', was built at a cost of £434 on a site in North Street, which had been part of the workhouse garden. This building, which was used for the boys' school, still stands as Mr. Willett's furniture

Cambell Senior School. Practical Science Room.

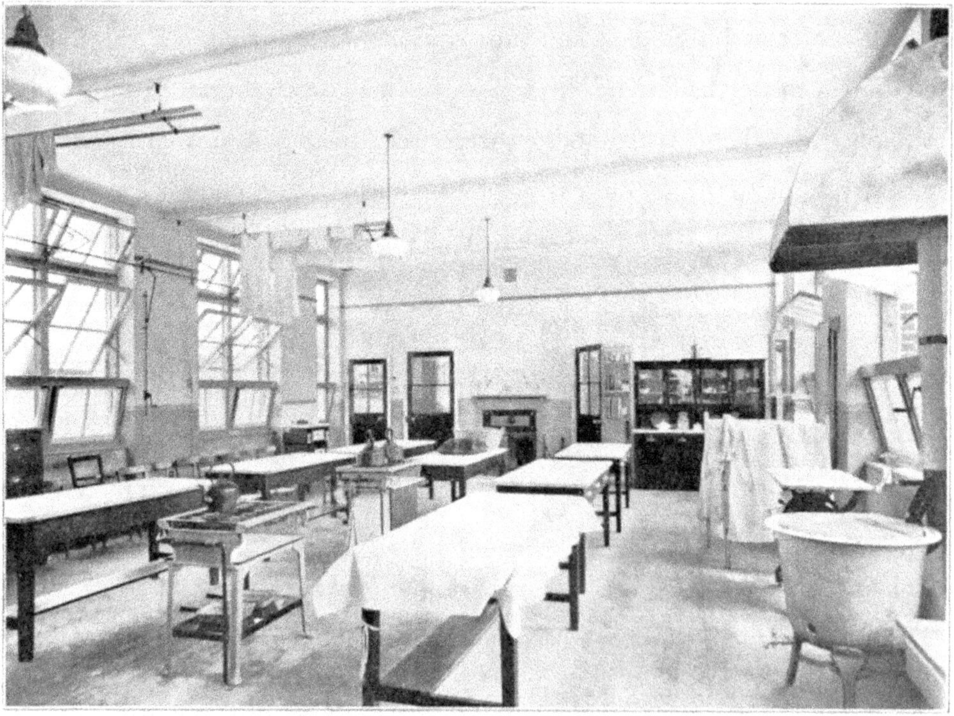

Cambell Senior School. Domestic Science Room.

warehouse. Modern shop windows hide the former schoolroom, but at the time of building two plans were submitted, one for a room with windows below the eaves, the other lighted only by a lantern. This latter was adopted and the lantern remains to this day.

By the time the new boys' school was opened, it is probable that the school in the workhouse disappeared. At all events, within a few years the Cambell endowments are recorded as being part of the revenue of the Church schools and the latter having become linked with the national society in 1824, took the name of the National School. A further room was built for 200 girls in 1848. Despite generous benefactors, the school had a troublesome life so that between 1850 and 1870 the buildings were reported to be inadequate, the discipline unsatisfactory, and the attendance of 80 to 90 disproportionately low for the size of the town. The Committee were hard put to it to keep solvent and avoid State aid, though, to show that the town was always mindful of its children, we find the first record of a school journey to the Zoo in 1866, when 1s. 0d. was spent on elephant rides for the boys.

Education was once more in the air. The Act of 1870 had thrown responsibilities on Church and State alike. Compulsory elementary education required more places and it was the Church which stepped forward to meet the need. Raising donations from the Bishop of Rochester's diocesan fund, similar funds in Essex, by parish subscriptions and by a grant of over £600 from the Department of Education, the present building was erected in Back Lane to accommodate 250 boys and 225 girls. This is the oldest building in the town still used for school purposes, and in design it stands midway between the single schoolroom of 1827 and the three-decker schools built by the School Board between 1890 and 1905. With the opening of the new building, a new staff was appointed, and the school once more became worthy of the town. For twenty years this school, in company with schools provided by the other denominations (for the Wesleyans, Congregationalists and Roman

Erkenwald Senior School. Assembly Hall and Principal Entrances.

Erkenwald Senior School. Quadrangle.

Catholics had all founded schools by 1890) met the needs of a rapidly growing Borough. In 1890, the total number of children in school was 1,771, of whom 1,046 were at the Church of England School, 356 at the Wesleyan, 215 at the Roman Catholic, and 154 at a school at Creeksmouth which had been opened in connexion with Lawes' Chemical Industry. The Department of Education was, however, demanding a further 500 places, for, between 1881 and 1891, the population had increased from 9,108 to 14,301, a rise of 57%. For nearly a hundred years the Churches had provided schooling for Barking's children, but now the task was too big, despite the fact that the National Schools were enlarged in 1888, when the yearly cost of education in them was stated to be only £1 6s. 9d. per head. Barking was rapidly changing from a village to an industrial borough and the State took up the work when the first School Board was elected in October, 1889. The growing population thrust ever increasing responsibilities on the Board which by 1903, when its powers were handed over to the Urban District Council, had become responsible for the education of a majority of Barking's children.

The School Board and Pre-War Development.

The years that follow 1890 are a record of the building of new schools to provide Barking with sufficient elementary accommodation. In 1892 the Gascoigne School was opened for 1,409 children, in 1896 the Northbury School for 1,714 children, and in 1904 the Westbury School for 1,569. These were all three-storey schools with a department on each storey, each department having its classrooms opening from a central hall. This design was in accordance with the prevailing conceptions, all these schools being extremely substantial and well built; but in 1912 the Ripple School was opened as one of the first bungalow schools in the country. Meanwhile, the needs of the outlying districts were met by the completion of the Castle School at Rippleside in 1898, and the Creeksmouth School in 1904.

Erkenwald Senior School. Hall.

Cambell Senior School. Hall.

The Barking schools before the war had kept pace not only with the increasing size of the town but also with changes in school design. The schools provided a sound primary education, based on reading, writing and arithmetic, but beyond this there was little demand for further educational facilities. Sir Michael Sadler in his report on Secondary and Higher Education in Essex, published in 1906, said of Barking, " that it would be undesirable to establish a secondary school and that at present there was no large enough nucleus of pupils for a higher elementary school," but he recommended the establishment of a manual training centre for boys, and that the three top standards in Northbury School should work as separate classes with their own curriculum, each class having no more than forty children. From these two ideas, that the hands as well as the brain are a medium of education, and that the senior children should be taught from a curriculum designed to meet the needs of adolescence, have sprung the most radical changes of recent years.

During the war, for the first time for fifty years there was no great increase in the population. This gave a breathing space for the Education Committee to survey the special needs of Barking's children, with the result that the Faircross Special School for physically and mentally defective children was completed in 1920, and the Park Modern Selective Central School in 1926. Meanwhile, the Essex Education Committee had opened the Abbey Secondary School so that whereas Barking before the war made no provision for children extending their full-time education beyond the age of fourteen, but relied upon her neighbours, within ten years of the end of the war she possessed a secondary and a central school, built on up-to-date lines with their own playing fields, which give an adequate opportunity for all capable of profiting from higher education. These schools have created a tradition for post primary education which has been well supported by the townsfolk despite the fact that twenty years previously it was the unanimous opinion of all connected with Barking that the time was not ripe for such developments.

Roding Junior School.   Principal Entrance Front.

Roding Junior School.   Quadrangle.

The Becontree Estate and Reorganisation.

In 1919, the London County Council began negotiations for the development of their housing estate in the Becontree area. By 1922 they had arranged for the purchase of 1,040 acres in the Borough of Barking, on which they planned to build 7,321 houses. Thus it was anticipated that the number of children to be educated in Barking schools would increase from 5,600 in 1925 to over 15,000 by 1934. At the same time, building by private enterprise and the housing activities of the Barking Council were ensuring that the expansion which had been the main feature of pre-war years was continuing with its former rapidity. The population increased from 35,523 in 1921 to 51,277 in 1931. Rarely has a Part III Education Authority had to shoulder such a responsibility or had so great an opportunity. A whole school system had to be planned and built for nearly 10,000 children. Not only schools but clinics and playing fields were necessary. New houses alone were not enough to challenge the slums: there had also to be an educational service that would create a new opportunity and a new hope.

The economies necessitated by the industrial collapse of 1920–1921 postponed the building of the first London County Council houses on Barking land until 1928, but, meanwhile, the Hadow Report had turned the attention of educationalists to the problem of teaching the older children in the elementary schools. With the development of post-primary schools to which children were drafted at 11, the senior standards of the elementary schools had the difficult task of teaching the general mass of children who were left. It was perhaps inevitable that the scholarship classes received first attention and hence that the top classes were denied the benefit of an education specially designed to meet their needs. The Report recommended that primary education should finish for all at 11, and that children should be promoted at that age to post-primary schools to meet their special abilities. The main body of children were to pass to Senior or Modern Schools where

Dawson Junior School.   Principal Entrance Front.

Dawson Junior School.   Children's Entrance and Assembly Hall.

a curriculum could be provided to cover not only the basic subjects of English and Arithmetic, but also craftwork and elementary science. It was hoped that by reducing the classes to 40 and providing specialisation among the teachers it would be possible to give more individual attention to the children, make better use of the staff and give new hope to backward children who had tended to be lost in the old schools. The Barking Education Committee at once realised the significance of this report. In the Becontree area it was possible from the first to organise all the schools on the new basis. In the older part of Barking the Committee courageously decided to reorganise prior to the development of the London County Council building programme. Two of the old departments at the Northbury and Gascoigne Schools were turned into senior girls' and boys' schools respectively, and the new Eastbury School, which had become necessary owing to the housing developments on the Eastbury Estate, was built as a Senior School to serve the eastern side of the town. To make adequate provision for handcraft and science, a new wing was added to the Gascoigne School, while the old handcraft rooms at Northbury School were converted to be domestic science rooms for the use of the girls.

These new buildings were sufficiently advanced for the Committee to put their scheme into effect after the Easter holiday, 1931. On that date all the provided schools were reorganised with the exception of the outlying Castle School which was destined to be closed after the opening of the Monteagle School on the new estate.

With the old schools reorganised, the Committee proceeded to push forward their building programme at Becontree where the London County Council were putting up houses so rapidly that in 1930 to 1931 over 100 houses were let a week, causing a weekly inflow of approximately 120 children. The full programme included three senior schools for children of 11–14, five junior schools for children of 9–11 and five infants' schools for children of 5–7.

Dawson Junior School. View under Verandah.

Dawson Junior School. A Classroom.

The three senior schools were so placed that while they could each draw pupils from a third of the estate they were also contiguous to the open belt where extra playing field accommodation will be provided. Semi-permanent buildings were first opened at the Cambell School in May, 1930, pending the completion of the infants' and senior departments which admitted children in May and September, 1931, respectively. On this site, which was named after the founder of the Free School, there are accommodated 880 seniors, 600 juniors and 400 infants. The semi-permanent buildings at the Erkenwald School were next completed by Easter, 1931, and occupied by juniors and infants until the latter moved over to similar buildings on the Roding site at Whitsuntide. Finally, these schools were reorganised in May, 1932, the Roding opening (besides the infants' department) two junior departments for boys and girls respectively, while the Erkenwald was reserved for senior pupils.

South of the railway line, two further schools, each with junior and infant accommodation, were erected, the semi-permanent accommodation at the Dawson School being opened in September, 1931, and the Monteagle School as a junior mixed and infants' school in August, 1932. The building progress has been such that few children coming into the district have had to wait long for their school places, and in a big majority of cases accommodation has been provided within a week of the child's arrival—no light task when it is remembered that within two years the Committee have built places for 5,900 children. This rapid development created difficult conditions both for teachers and parents to whom the highest praise is due: to the former for the way in which they have taught in half-built schools without halls or proper playgrounds, and to the latter for cheerful co-operation at times when the only approach to school has been over builders' planks across a field of mud.

Much remains to be done. The last of the junior and infants' schools, the Dorothy Barley School, will be begun in the autumn and the last of the senior schools on site L. early in next year. The plans for both these schools represent improvements gained by the experience of previous buildings. Arrangements for adequate clinical accommodation are under way and land for playing-fields on the open belts has been reserved. The expenditure has been heavy despite the closest regard for economy, and the Committee have done all in their power to distribute the burden of it over a number of years.

The future lies with the teachers and citizens of Barking. Each school has its own character to develop and its own part to play in the social growth of the borough. The Committee believe that they have built a school system which, within its dimensions, is second to none; they know that these schools are served by teachers, both young and old, who are fully capable of making the best of their opportunity and they trust that the public will reap the full advantage of the facilities which have been provided for Barking children.

The Development of School Design.

By C. J. DAWSON, F.R.I.B.A.,
Architect to the Authority.

Changes in Design, 1890—1925.

The development of Elementary School planning in England since 1870 is well illustrated by the school buildings in Barking. The accompanying plans and photographs demonstrate how changes in educational and medical theory have influenced school design. The earliest plans (figs. 1 and 2) which are those of Gascoigne and Westbury Schools, respectively, show the type of building prevalent for a period of 20 years commencing about 1889. It was in general favour because it enabled the head teacher to see into every classroom when seated at the desk in the assembly hall. In large schools it was repeated on three floors, the infants', girls' and boys' departments being on the ground, first and second floors respectively. A teachers' private room and lavatory were provided for each department in the mezzanine floors between the children's cloakrooms.

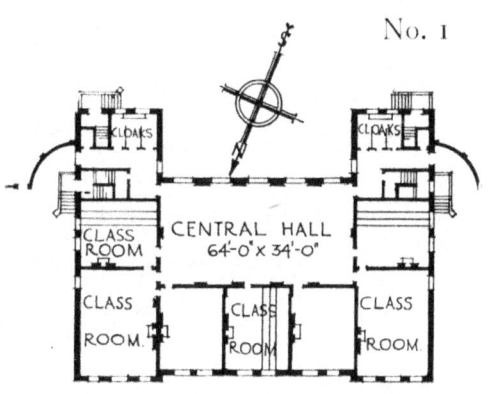

Gascoigne School. Accommodation **1272**.

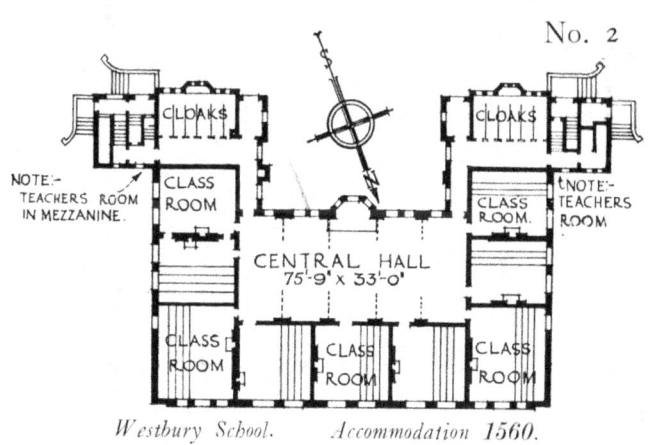

Westbury School. Accommodation **1560**.

The difficulty of obtaining satisfactory

23

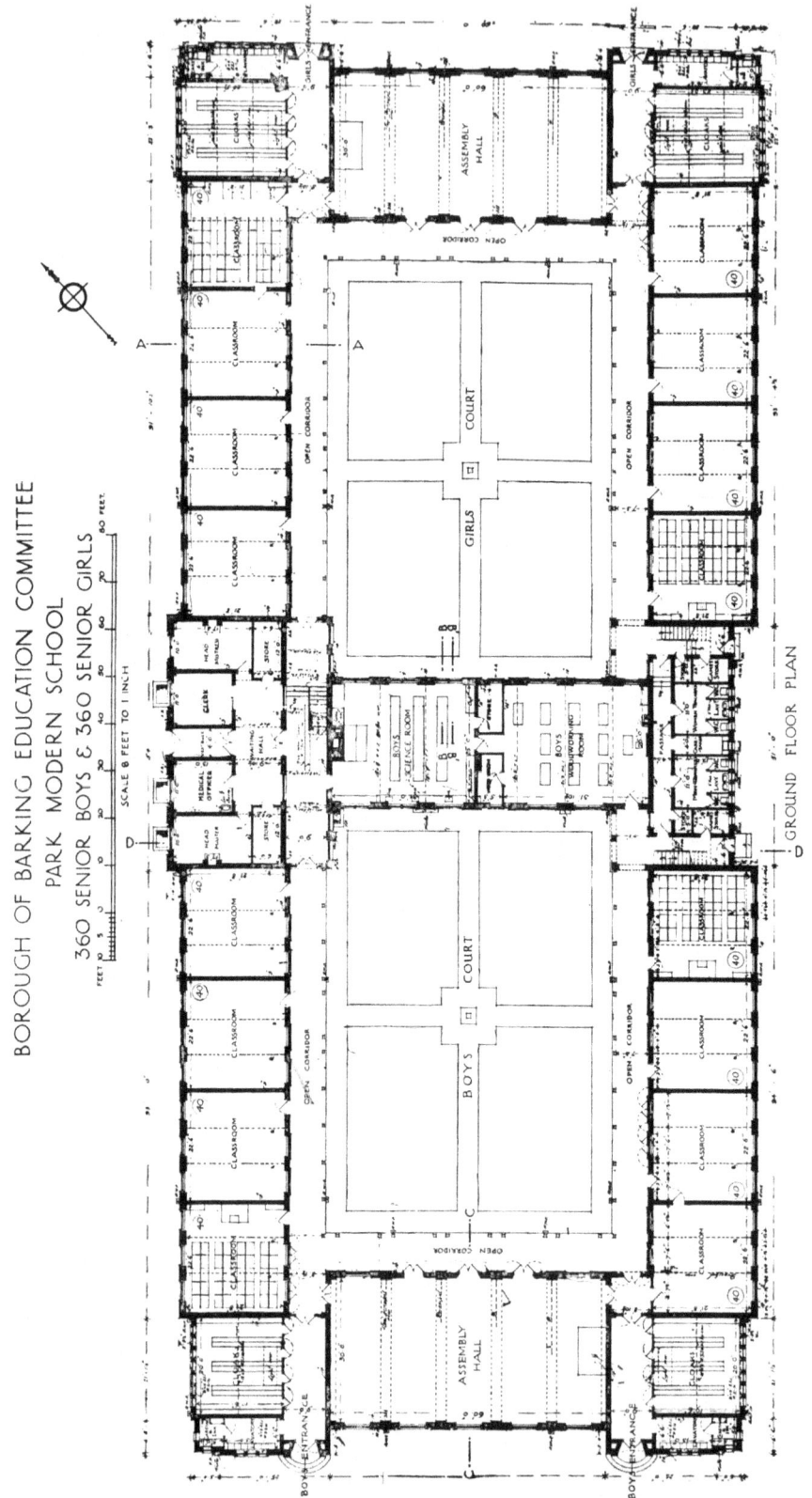

independent through ventilation of the class rooms and halls, the increased use of the halls for school activities which made it difficult for the Head Teacher to work there during school hours, and also distracted the attention of the children in the classrooms, caused the

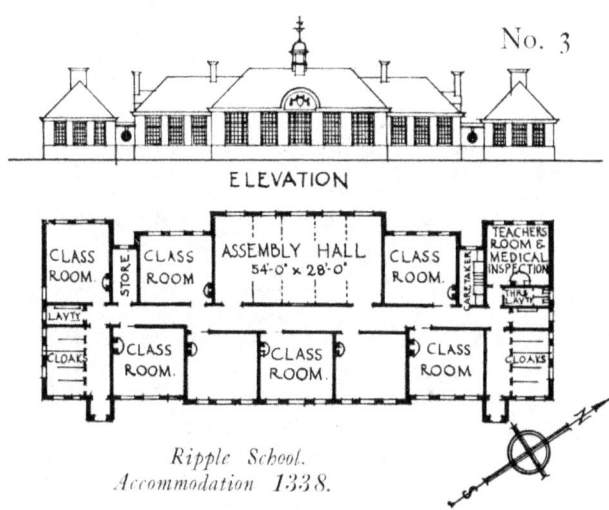

Ripple School. Accommodation 1338.

abandonment of this plan and the substitution of a new type shown in figs. 3 and 4, which is the design of one of the three blocks of Ripple School, erected in 1912. In this school, each department is accommodated in a separate single storey block in which the cross-ventilation and lighting of the classrooms and halls is obtained by windows above the level of the corridor roofs as shown in the sketch below.

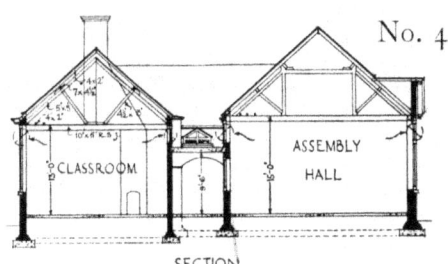

The next development was not until 1920, when the Faircross Special School was built. This school, which accommodates 320 physically and mentally defective children, represents a distinct break with all previous types and consists of a series of connected units each comprising two classrooms with its own cloakroom, lavatory and entrance lobby, all corridors being eliminated. The assembly hall, which is in the centre of the building at right angles to the main block, besides being cross-ventilated and lighted, has a kitchen and scullery at one end for the purpose of providing children with dinners. This type of plan enables the two sides of each classroom to be thrown open to the air.

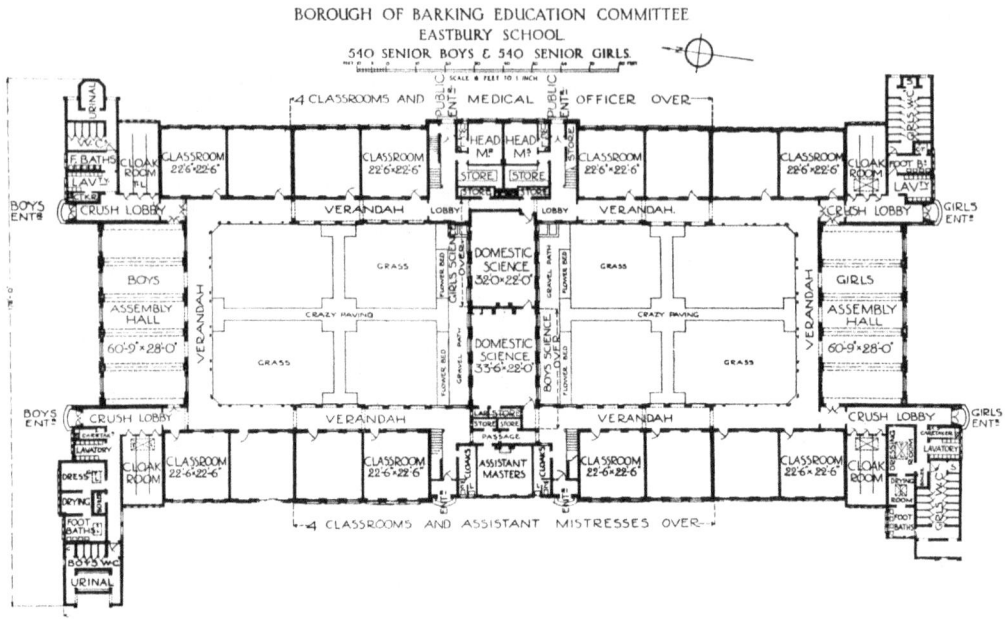
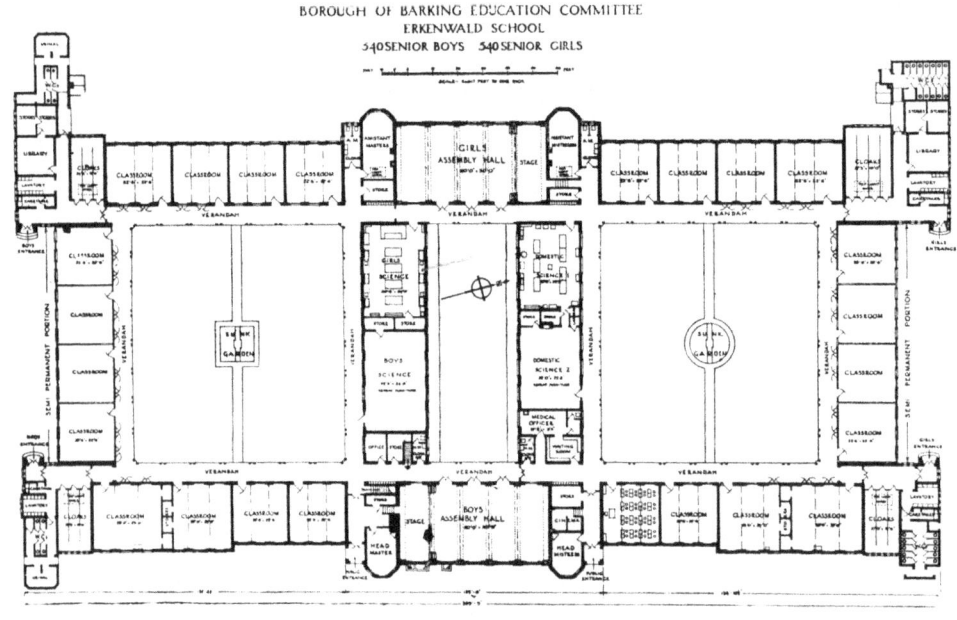

Quadrangle : Open Verandah Plan. The first school in the town to be built on the quadrangle open verandah plan was the Park Modern School, accommodating 360 boys and 360 girls. A great deal of consideration was given to this plan before it was adopted owing to the doubt as to whether children and teachers would suffer in health owing to exposure on the open verandahs when passing from room to room. Experience has shown that the general health of scholars and teachers alike has in no way suffered so that this quadrangle open verandah type has been adopted for all schools erected by the Committee since that date. A woodwork and a metalwork room for boys have been added as an annexe to the main building, together with spray baths for both boys and girls, for use in connexion with the schools playing fields.

Reorganisation caused an interesting addition to the Gascoigne School, when the obsolete latrines and open play sheds were demolished to make room for the erection of a new three-storey annexe of six classrooms with cloakrooms, lavatories and staircases, connected to the main building at first-floor level by an enclosed bridge. A new manual training building with two rooms for metal and wood work respectively, and new latrines for all departments were also erected at the same time.

The Becontree Programme. With the growth of the Becontree Estate and the reorganisation of the schools within the town, it was necessary to commence building work on a number of school sites almost simultaneously, with the result that the Eastbury, Cambell, Roding, Erkenwald, Dawson and Monteagle Schools, providing 7,700 places, have been designed, built and occupied during the last three years, 1929-32. Also during this period plans have been prepared for building two more schools, the Dorothy Barley and School L., which will provide 2,160 places, making a total of 9,860 school places.

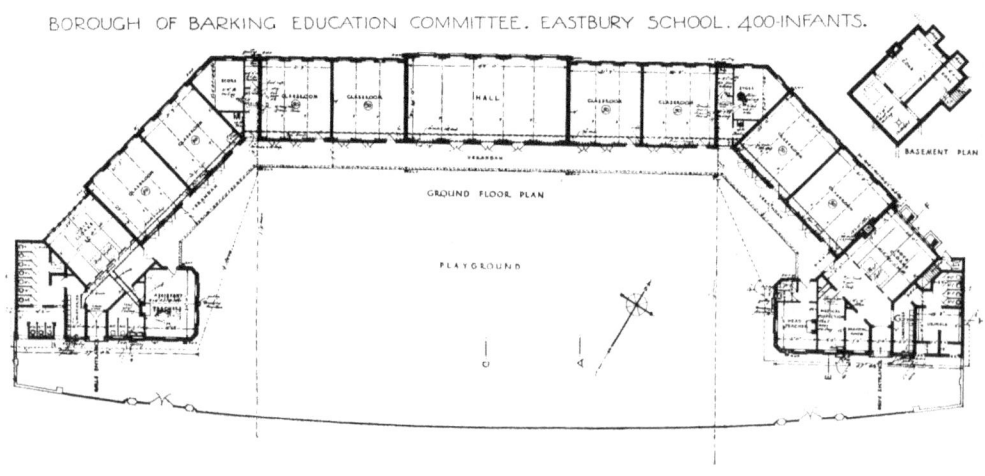

As the sites for all these schools were between four and five acres and as further playing-field accommodation was scheduled on the open belt, it was decided to plan all the senior and junior departments on the open verandah quadrangle type as well as the infants' departments at the Monteagle and Dawson Schools. This decision allowed for the maximum standardisation of materials and fittings. The other infants' departments have the halls and classrooms in line, with the open verandahs facing south, the inclined wings of the building forming a sun-trap which protects the playgrounds as far as possible from northerly winds.

Semi-Permanent Buildings. A portion of each school building is built of semi-permanent construction. This is due partly to the need for rapid construction, but also to ensure elasticity of organisation in the event of changes in child population or in educational method. At the Cambell School, a semi-permanent building to accommodate 600 children in twelve classrooms, with cloakrooms and lavatories, was erected as a separate unit, while eight classrooms at Erkenwald and six each at Roding, Dawson and Monteagle Junior Schools were built in this manner. These semi-permanent buildings consist of walls and partitions formed of timber framing in sections bolted together so that they can be taken down and re-erected on another site. This framing is set up on brick dwarf walls, the inside of the framed walls and both sides of the partitions being lined with plywood and the ceilings with "Ten-test." On the outside the walls are covered with "Ten-test" rendered in cement and the roofs with corrugated asbestos sheeting. The floors are laid with batten flooring on joists and the windows in each case are similar to those in the permanent buildings.

Planning. Eastbury and Cambell Schools have each two main blocks of buildings, one for senior boys and girls and the other for infants. The Erkenwald School has one main block only for senior boys and girls,

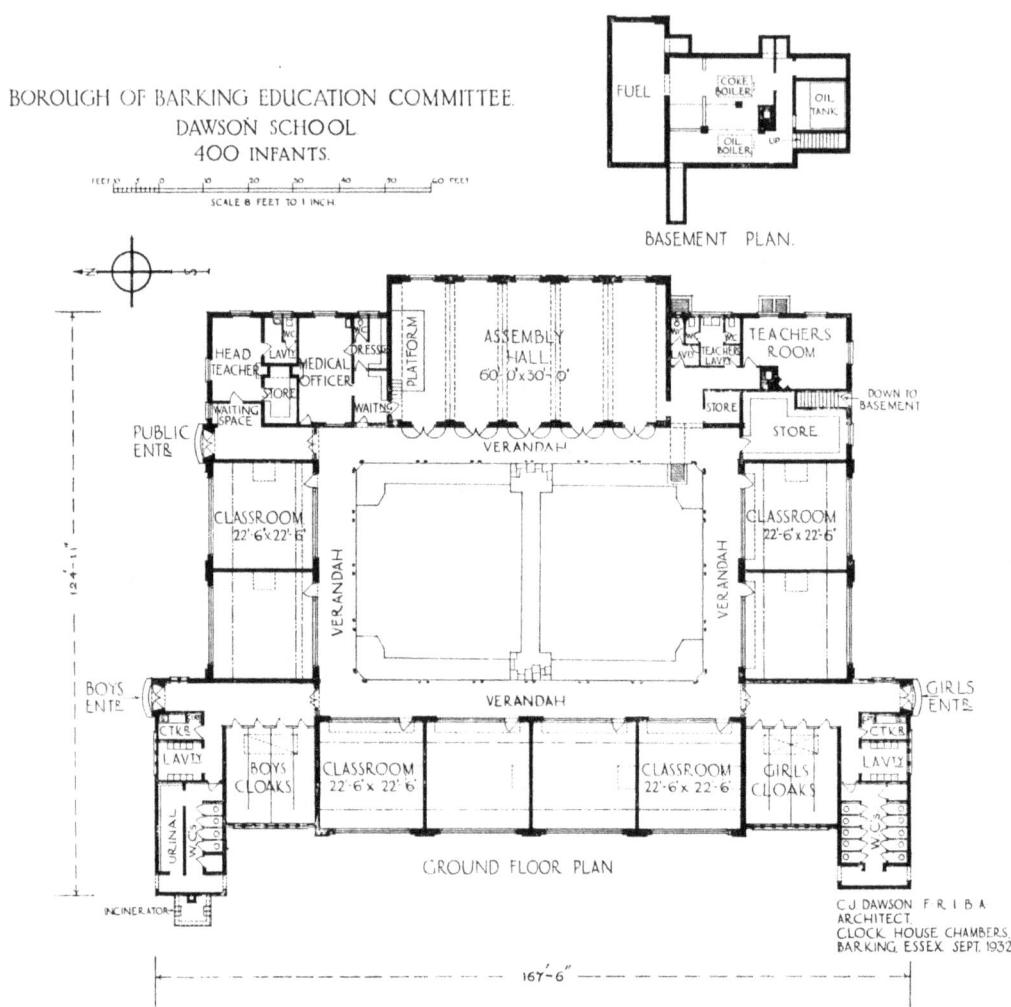

while the Dawson, Monteagle and Roding Schools have each two blocks, one for junior boys and girls and the other for infants. The handicraft rooms at the Eastbury, Cambell and Erkenwald Schools are in a small separate block adjacent to the boys' department in each case. In all these schools the children's latrines are not isolated in blocks away from the school building, as was the previous practice, but are attached to the lavatory and cloakroom wings at the corners of the buildings. Isolation is no longer necessary, owing to the improvement in sanitary fittings, and the plans show that there is ample air passage between the latrines and the main building.

The provisional plans for the Dorothy Barley School with two departments for juniors and one for infants, and for the senior school on Site L. show modifications of the basic design. In the junior block two large classrooms have been provided in each department for practical work, each fitted with a sink. In the infants' school the hall has been displaced by two playrooms, one of which has a folding partition so that a portion can be shut off for medical inspection, and a babies' room has been designed with its own entrance lobby, cloakroom, lavatory and latrines. The folding doors of this room open on to the verandah and gardens. The senior departments on Site L. have three large classrooms, each with a sink and store, for subsidiary craft work. Two of these and the special subjects rooms are of semi-permanent construction. It has also been possible to use the roof space over the head teachers' rooms as a library, which will be lighted by dormer windows.

Although these schools have not yet been built, their designs are of peculiar interest as they represent the first schools to be planned since reorganisation. The increased accommodation for subsidiary handicrafts in the Senior School, the provision of two large classrooms for handwork in each department of the Junior School, and the Free Activity Rooms in the Infants' School, are the outcome of practical teaching experience during the eighteen months which have elapsed since reorganisation.

BOROUGH OF BARKING EDUCATION COMMITTEE
RODING SCHOOL
500 JUNIOR BOYS, 500 JUNIOR GIRLS

BOROUGH OF BARKING EDUCATION COMMITTEE
DAWSON SCHOOL
400 JUNIOR BOYS, 400 JUNIOR GIRLS

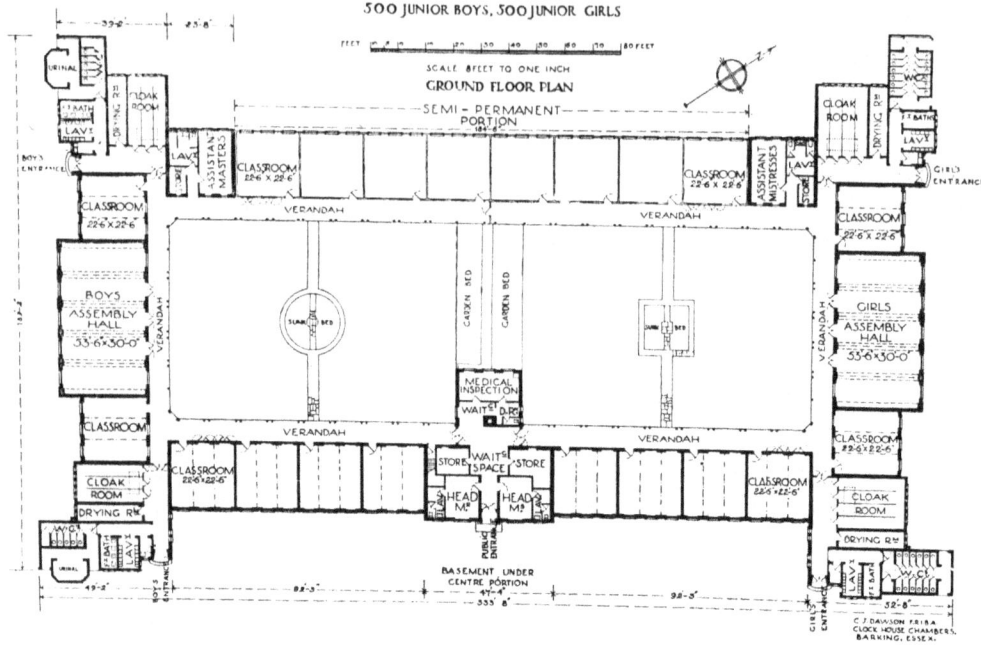

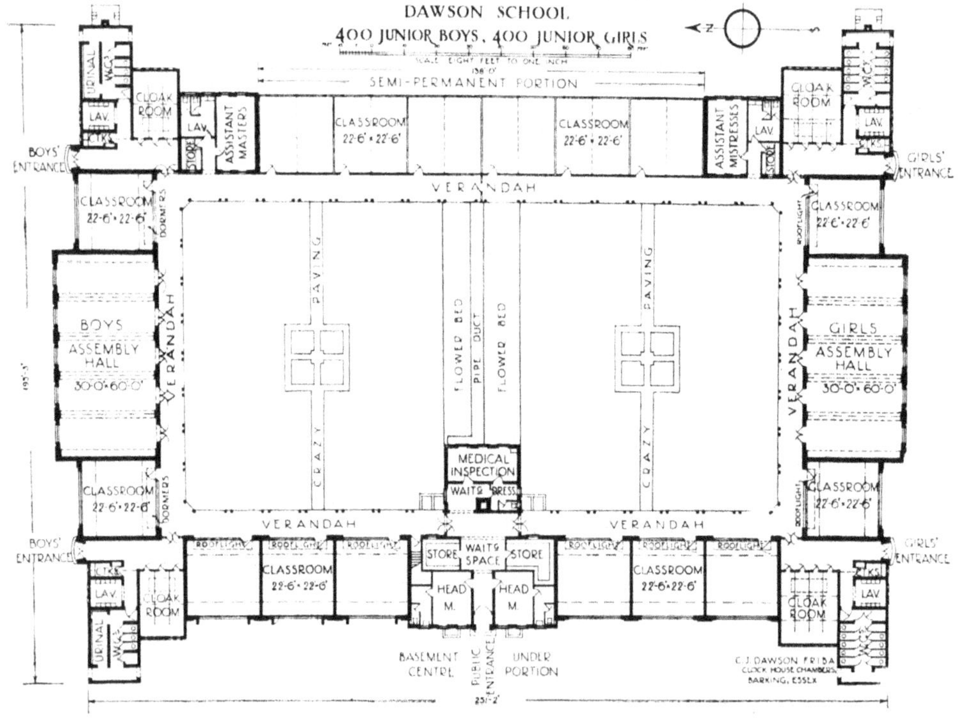

Classrooms. As the building scheme progressed an important development took place in classroom design. Drawing A. represents a section of a classroom at the Roding and the previous schools, Drawing B. a section of a classroom at the Dawson and subsequent schools.

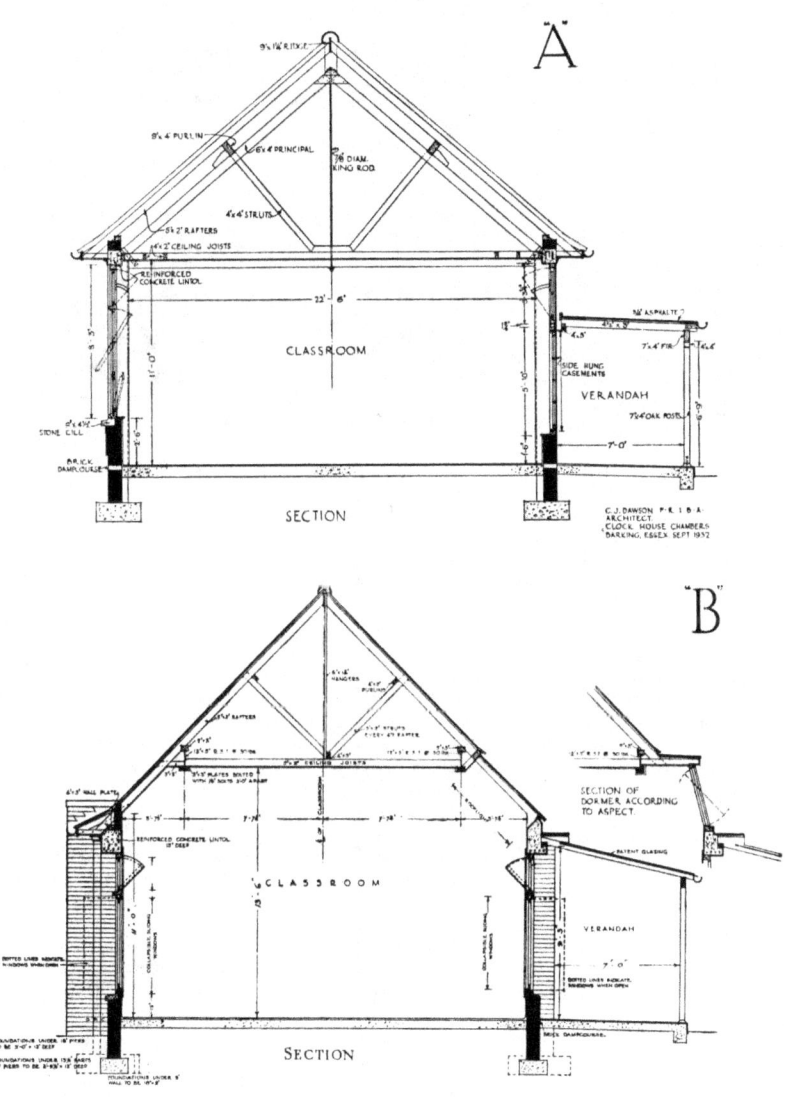

The advantages of the new classrooms lie in the improved lighting and simplified ventilation obtained by the use of folding sash windows and hoppers. In cold weather the folding sashes can be closed on one or both sides of the

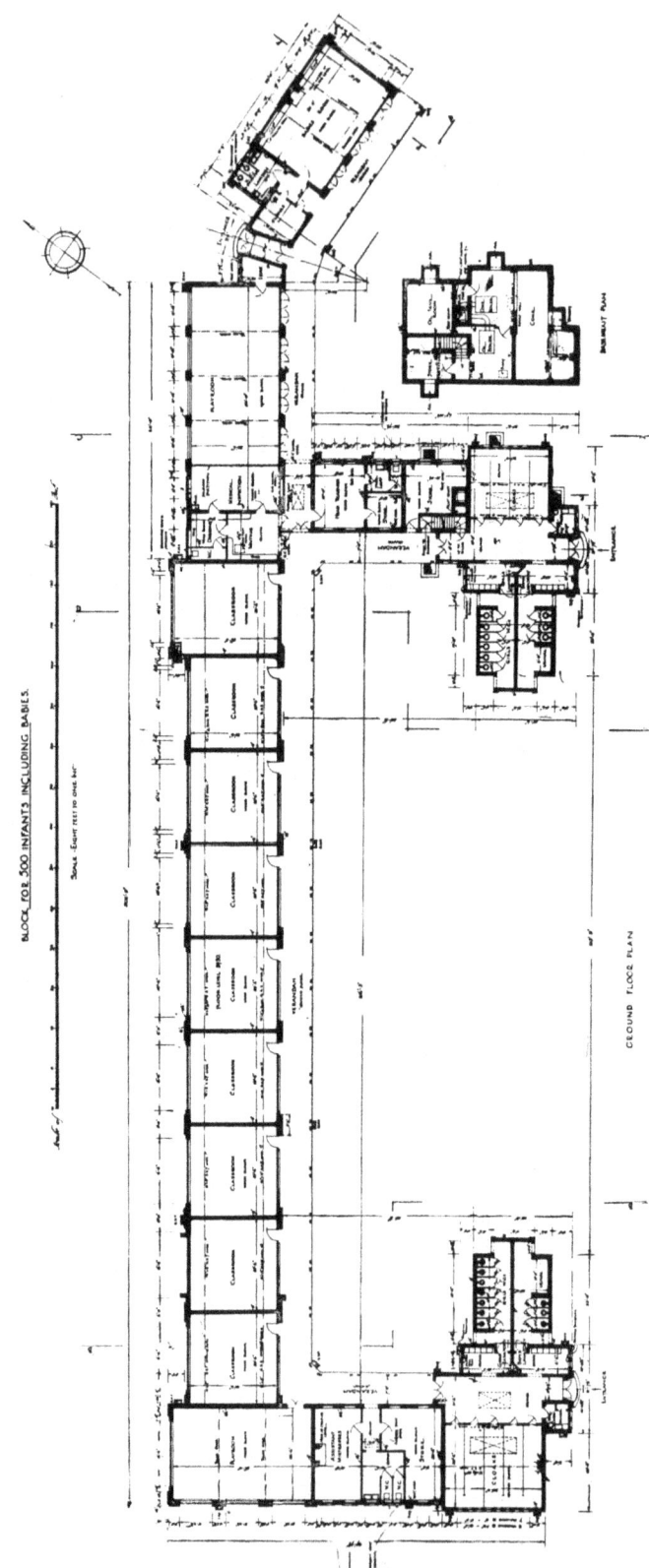

classroom and the hoppers left open as they are so placed and constructed as to provide an ample flow of fresh air without a direct draught on the children. The continuous roof lights above the verandah roofs ensure effective lighting and when it is impracticable for these to face in a northerly direction sloping dormers with opening sashes are provided.

Heating. The heating of all these schools is by radiators and pipes fed from low pressure hot water boilers in the basement heating chambers, open fires which were provided in earlier types of classrooms being omitted, as, owing to the ample cross-ventilation available in classrooms with windows on both sides, they were not necessary for ventilation purposes. The heating boilers are in duplicate, one being oil, the other coke fed; owing to the long runs of pipes in one-storey buildings, duplicate accelerating pumps are also provided. The cold water mains both to and from the storage tanks are as far as practicable underground to avoid frost, while the tank rooms, whether they are in the roof spaces or in towers, have small electric stoves, with a central switch and red " tell-tale " lamp in the corridor beneath.

Lavatories and Latrines. The lavatory basins have been arranged so that the children wash under running water to avoid the risk of contagion. In the latrines each fitting has its own flushing tank filled on the gravity system by a main tank fitted with a ballcock at each end of the range. This system ensures a rapid filling of each tank.

Decorations. Particular attention has been given to the interior decoration of the schools for the purpose of brightening and giving individuality to the various rooms. In the infants' departments, the furniture is coloured in various shades of cellulose enamel.

Quadrangles. The quadrangles are laid out with grass, stone paved paths and flower beds, the upkeep of which is part of the work of the children.

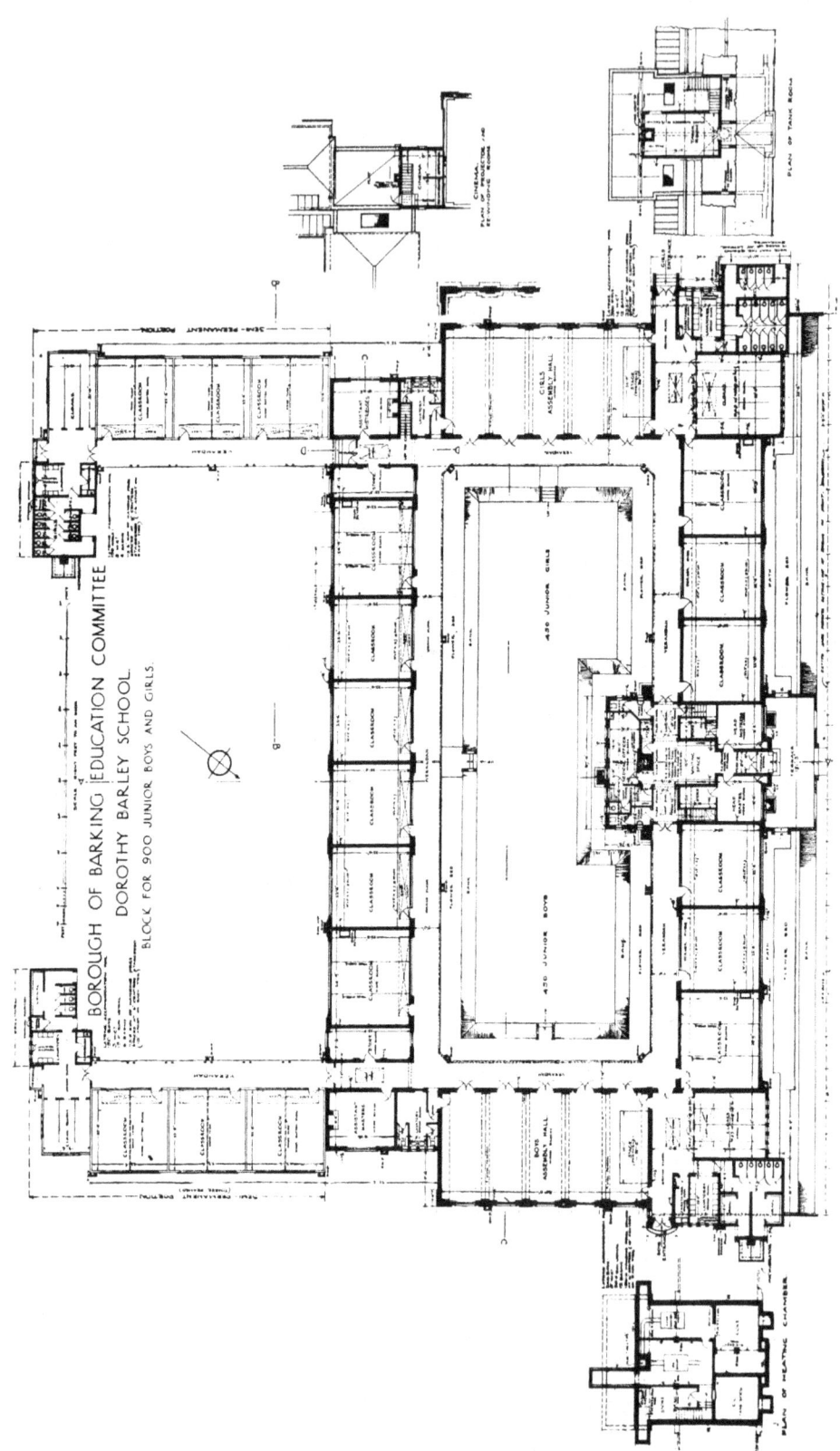

The Barking schools have been built to meet modern educational requirements, with adaptability of accommodation and at a reasonable cost. No plan can be final, for new ideas demand new buildings. A generation ago the Board of Education advised a northerly aspect for classrooms; to-day the aim of the school architect is to catch the maximum of sun and fresh air; to-morrow will reveal some new need. But if the schools can show no finality, the story of their erection is an interesting record of fifty years' progress in design.

———◆———

The Architect desires to express his appreciation of the keen and helpful interest taken by the Director of Education in the planning of the new schools, and also of the assistance received from his Partners and Staff in designing and supervising the several buildings.

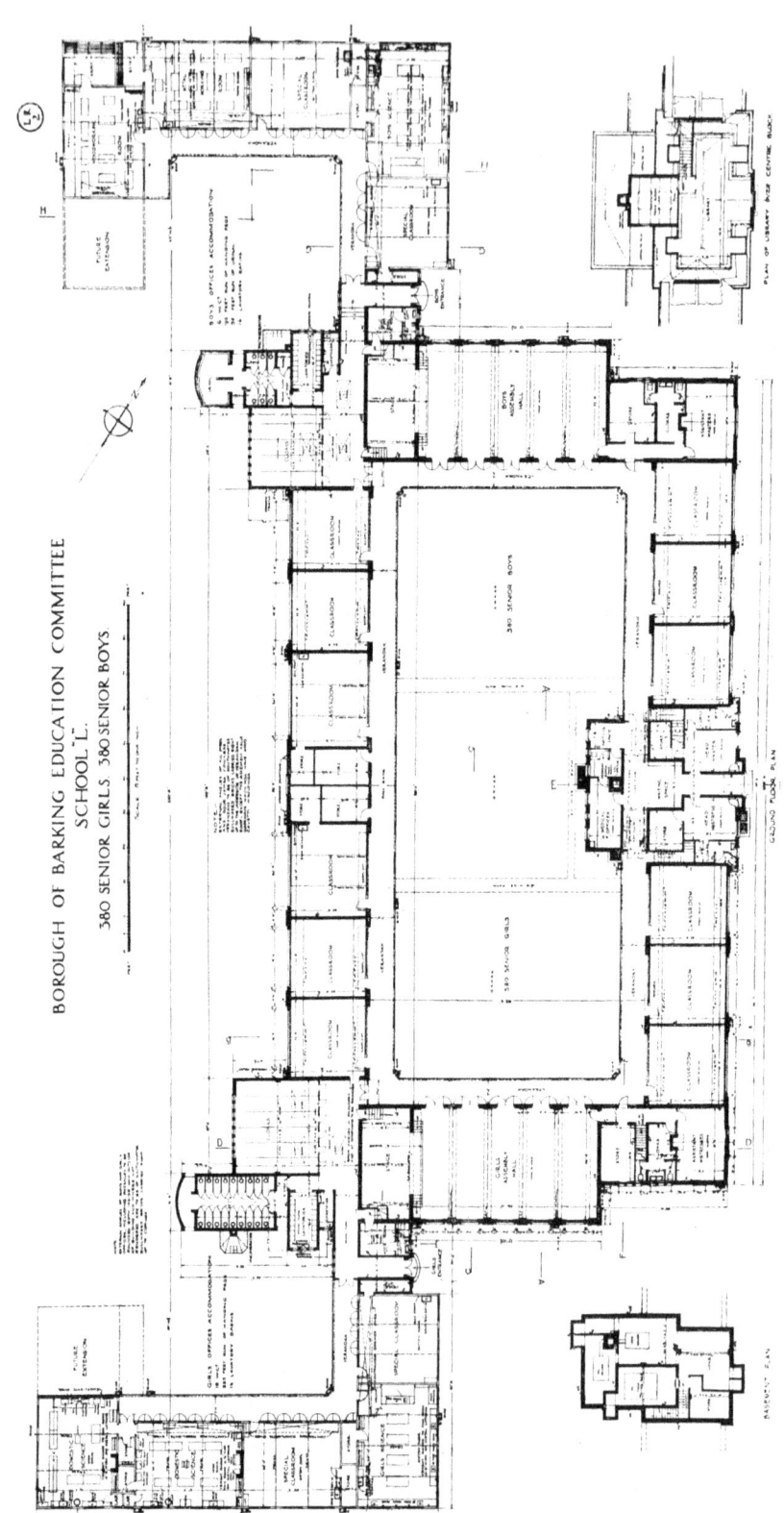

ACCOMMODATION AND COST OF SCHOOLS.

The Cost given below includes Heating, Lighting, Drainage, Boundary Walls and Fencing but excludes Site, Furniture, Tar-paving and Caretaker's House.

Name of School.	Accommodation.	Cost. Total.	Cost. Per Place.	
		£	£ s. d.	
EASTBURY SCHOOL. Senior Boys and Girls and Infants (Built by Contract)	1,480	41,250	27 17 5	Contract Amount.
CAMBELL SCHOOL. Senior Boys and Girls and Infants (Built by Contract)	1,240	41,829	33 14 8	Contract Amount.
ERKENWALD SCHOOL. Senior Boys and Girls (Built by Direct Labour)	1,080	38,664	35 16 0	Surveyor's Estimate.
RODING SCHOOL. Junior Boys and Girls and Infants (Built by Direct Labour)	1,500	43,026	28 13 8	Surveyor's Estimate.
DAWSON SCHOOL. Junior Boys and Girls and Infants (Built by Direct Labour)	1,200	39,723	33 1 8	Surveyor's Estimate.
MONTEAGLE SCHOOL. Junior Boys and Girls and Infants (Built by Direct Labour)	1,200	40,614	33 16 11	Surveyor's Estimate.
DOROTHY BARLEY SCHOOL. Junior Boys and Girls and Infants (Not yet built)	1,400	41,428	29 11 10	Architect's Estimate.

KEY PLAN OF SCHOOLS.

Schools on the 90th Anniversary – 6th October 2022

Dawson:

The school closed in 1966, the remaining pupils were transferred to either Dorothy Barley School or Cambell School. The site subsequently became known as Bifrons Annexe. The buildings were used by Mayesbrook Secondary School from 1970 until its closure in 1989.

Erkenwald:

The school amalgamated with Parsloes Manor School and Mayesbrook Secondary School to create Sydney Russell Comprehensive School in 1990. The site in Marlborough Road is now a centre offering education and support to those struggling to attend mainstream school.

Roding:

Still open on two sites, the original Hewett Road site and Cannington Road. St Teresa's Catholic School after sharing part of the Hewett Road site, took over the Bowes Road site.

Cambell (now known as James Cambell Primary school), Eastbury and Monteagle are still serving the community.

The Archives & Local Studies Centre at Valence House Museum in the London Borough of Barking & Dagenham is the source and inspiration for many local heritage projects. When volunteers working there wish to develop and expand topics of significant local historical interest they are encouraged with the generous support of the professional staff.

This publication is a scanned reproduction of the book originally published in 1932 and is being republished on the 6th October 2022 on the 90th Anniversary of its original release.

All money raised from this publication will go to fund future projects.

www.ingramcontent.com/pod-product-compliance
Lightning Source LLC
Chambersburg PA
CBHW070339120526
44590CB00017B/2955